HTML & HTML5: T beginners guide to learn the HTML, HTML5 and basic CSS Fundamentals

Table of Contents

HTML & HTML5: The ultimate beginners guide to learn the HTML, HTML5 and basic CSS Fundamentals 1

Table of Contents 2

Introduction 4

Chapter 1: What Is HTML? 6

How to Create a Web Page Using HTML 7

HTML Tags 9

Empty Tags or Void Elements 10

The Essential HTML Tags 11

HTML Tag 11

Head Tag 12

Body Tag 12

Title Tag 13

Chapter 2: HTML Visible and Common Elements and Attributes 14

Headings 14

Paragraphs 16

Basic Formatting 18

Bolding and Italicization 19

Mark, Sub, Sup, and Small 20

Ins and Del 20

Attributes 20

More on ASCII Characters 23

Links 24

Target Attribute 26

Images 26

Image File Locations 27

Alt Attribute 29

Basic Image Resizing 29

Style Attribute 30

Tables 31

Lists 34

List Style Type...36
List Child..38
Description List 39
Adding Comments 41
Chapter 3: A Quick and Condense Discussion about CSS 43
The Style Attribute or Inline Styles.......................................43
The Style Tag or Internal Stylesheet.....................................44
Styling Using the Element's Name as a Selector.............45
Styling Using the Element's ID as a Selector 46
Styling Using Class as a Selector 47
Styling Using the Element Tag and Class as a Selector ...49
Styling Using the Group Selectors 50
Using a Separate File for CSS or External Style Sheet 52
Multiple CSS Links and Declarations 53
CSS Properties and Compatibility...55
Chapter 4: Last Things You Need to Know..............................57
Block and Inline Level Elements..57
Changing from Block to Inline and Vice Versa 58
Grouping Tags and HTML5 Semantic Tags.......................58
Benefits of Semantic Tags versus Grouping Tags............60
SEO and Semantic Tags 60
Basic Web Page Structure..61
Conclusion and for Further Learning......................................66
A Quick Discussion on Static Pages 66
A Quick Discussion on Responsive Pages and Client Side
Scripting 66
A Quick Discussion on Dynamic Pages and Server Side
Scripting...67

Introduction

Thank you for downloading this book.

Why study HTML? Learning HTML would enable you to become more familiar with how websites work and how browsers display a page. Alternatively, if you are aiming to become a web developer it is must. If you want to learn PHP, ASP, or even JavaScript, you will need to learn it as a prerequisite.

HTML is THE language of the internet, so learning it could get you far in e-commerce.

Whether you just want to learn it for learning's sake or you want to use this book as a reference to pass your HTML certification, you will surely understand and know how HTML works and how you can create a web page from scratch after reading this book.

This introduction will not be long; after all, you got a lot to read after this. Take note that HTML and CSS code examples will be in the Courier New font, the supposed result of those codes will be in Times New Romans (though some might not), and explanations and discussions will be left in regular font, which is Georgia.

The book is aimed at beginners or to aspiring web developers. Nevertheless, it could be useful to advanced developers as a reference book for teaching HTML.

Have fun learning HTML!

Chapter 1: What Is HTML?

Surely, you already have an idea what is HTML, what it does, and why it is essential in the World Wide Web. Nevertheless, for formality's sake and to make sure that everyone is on the same page, the definition of HTML will be discussed briefly below.

HTML or Hyper Text Markup Language is the standard markup language used on the internet. It enables website owners to provide their visitors with web pages to view. Each page on the internet is composed of HTML. But of course, there are exceptions.

By the way, take note that HTML is not a programming language. And do not think that it is a complex language to master; it is not. Unlike the files from most programming languages, HTML files do not need to be compiled in order to be viewed. However, for them to be viewed, you will need a browser.

Web developers just simply open a browser and access the file from it. On the other hand, to write an HTML page, a typical text editing program like Microsoft Window's Notepad can suffice.

There are programs that can do HTML for you such as Adobe's Dreamweaver and Website Builder apps from hosting websites, so why do you still need to learn HTML? Unfortunately, those programs can limit your website or web page's design. Also, to take advantage of Dreamweaver's full potential or other HTML creation programs, they will require you to edit and code HTML as well. Nevertheless, if you just want to create simple web pages, there is no problem with depending to those programs.

Those are just a few of the things you need to know before you proceed reading this book. Just to set things straight, the book will talk about HTML5. Any obsolete elements or methods in HTML will be not discussed or will only be lightly explained if it is essential for you to have a better understanding of the subject.

How to Create a Web Page Using HTML

Open a text editor on your computer. If your computer runs on Microsoft Windows, you can use Notepad. But in case you are not that happy with Notepad, it is a good idea to use Notepad++ instead. Notepad++ is a free program that acts like notepad, but has advanced features that are geared towards web developers and programmers alike. HTML development is easy with this tool.

If you have a Mac, you can use TextMate – the program is free to download from the internet. Also, it has some features that Notepad++ has – which can help you code HTML easier. On the other hand, if your computer is running on Linux, you have an abundance of text editors to choose from. Just check your package manager, and get one. By the way, most people use gEdit and Emacs Editor.

Now, you are ready to go. Type the following in your text editor.

```
<!DOCTYPE html>

<html>

<body>

<h1>This is my first web page!</h1>

<p>Hello world!</p>

</body>

</html>
```

Save the document with any name that you want. However, it is essential that you indicate the correct file extension. Since you are going to save an HTML file, it must have the file extension .html or .htm. It is preferable that you use the latter.

In case you fail to indicate the correct file extension, your system and web browser(s) will be unable to recognize the file as an HTML page. In case you did indicate the right extension, you can now open the file on your browser. The browser will now display something like this.

This is my first web page!

Hello world!

Now, you might have some questions in mind. Where are the ones that are enclosed in the angled brackets? Those are html tags.

HTML Tags

The ones in the enclosed angled brackets or Chevrons are called HTML element tags. HTML element tags usually come in pairs. The first one in the pair is called the start, starting, or opening tag, and the second in the pair is called end, ending, or closing tag. The main difference between them, as you might have already noticed, is that the closing tag has a forward slash with it.

Take note that if your closing tag does not have the slash symbol in it, the browser will consider it as a starting tag. There are, however, some element tags that do not require a closing tag.

HTML element tags are the ones that guide or tell the browser how your page should be displayed and other miscellaneous stuff that your browser needs to know about the page. For example, the h1 tag told your browser that the content inside it, which is 'This is my first web page!', should be displayed as a header. On the other hand, the !DOCTYPE tag told the browser that your page is an HTML5 compliant web page or what version of HTML was used to write the page.

In HTML, numerous tags exist. However, it does not mean that you need to memorize all of them in one go in order to create web pages. At first, you just need to understand the core tags that should be present in your web pages. And they are !DOCTYPE, html, title, script, head, body, and footer.

!DOCTYPE is not actually an HTML tag. It is more like a declaration to inform your browser what version of HTML it would need to expect. Since this book focuses on HTML5, all the examples that will be written here will have or use <!DOCTYPE html>. If you place that on your page, the browser will understand that you are writing using HTML5.

Take note, the doc type declaration must be placed on the first line of your page and/or before the html tag. Your web page will still work even if you do not declare the version of your web page. However, it is far better to adhere to standard practice.

Empty Tags or Void Elements

As mentioned a while ago, some tags are not required to have closing tags. Those are called empty tags, self-closing tags, or void elements. They do not need to have content or they are incapable of having one. One good example of an empty tag is the <hr> tag. Try to include it on your document. Remember, it does not need to have a closing tag. However, you have the option to place a space and a forward slash before the less than sign – like this <hr />. Getting used to placing that slash is good practice if you desire to learn XML or XHTML, too.

Save the document and open it on your browser. If you have done it correctly, a horizontal line will appear on your page.

Some empty tags will be mentioned in this book. But as a reference, here is a complete list of void elements in HTML: <area>, <base>, <br>, <col>, <command>, <embed>, <hr>, <img>, <input>, <keygen>, <link>, <meta>, <param>, <source>, <track>, and <wbr>.

The Essential HTML Tags

In HTML, there are three core tags that you will always need to use in every page that you will create. Each tag has an important purpose. Most websites that you will find on the internet will always have those tags. In case they are not present on the document, the browser may generate them for the page.

Before you proceed, take note that you can write your HTML tags in lowercase, UPPERCASE, Proper Case or even CaMeL CaSe. HTML tags are not case sensitive. However, other types of markup language are strict and require lowercase (e.g. XHTML, XML). Due to that, it is recommendable that you practice writing in lowercase. Not only it will prevent you from adjusting when you start learning other markup languages, but it is easier to read and type in lowercase when it comes to HTML.

HTML Tag

The html tag tells the browser that everything inside its starting tag and closing tag are part of the HTML page that you want to show. In case that you forget to place the starting and closing html tags in your web page, the browser will automatically assume that all the content in your web page is inside an html tag.

Head Tag

The head tag houses most of the metadata for your document. A few of those tags are <title>, <style>, <base>, <meta>, <link>, and <script>.

Body Tag

The body tag will contain most of the visible elements that you will want to show in your page. The body tag contains your paragraphs, images, hyperlinks, and other elements.

Placing multiple body tags in your document will be useless. Most browsers, especially Google Chrome, will only consider the first starting body tag and last closing body tag in your document. Everything else in between those tags will be considered within the body.

Of course, you might have already thinking about how can you add pictures, links, and text in your web page? Well, again, you can do it by placing tags. And if you are going to add visible content in your page, you must make sure that you insert it inside the body tag of your web page.

By the way, each type of content requires different HTML tags. For example, if you want to insert a picture, you will need to place an <img> tag in your document. If you want to add a paragraph, you will need to type your paragraph inside the <p> tag. If you want to create a heading, you will need to place the line inside the <h1> – <h6> tag (there are six headings in HTML).

Title Tag

This is not included in the essential tags that you must indicate in your HTML file. But it is almost recommended to indicate the title of your page in your document. The <title> tag should be placed inside the <head> tag. The title that you will place in it will determine the title that will appear on the tab or title bar of the browser once your page is viewed. In case that you did not place a title in your page, most browsers will just use the URL of the page as the title of your web page.

Chapter 2: HTML Visible and Common Elements and Attributes

Here comes the meat of the discussion. This chapter will discuss almost all the basic elements that you need to know in order for you to show your content in your webpage. Expect that this chapter will be a bit longer than the rest. Each HTML tag will be discussed in detailed and multiple HTML development tips will be scattered around each section.

Headings

The HTML specification allows a web developer to use six different types of headings – <h1>, <h2>, <h3>, <h4>, <h5>, and <h6>. Any text placed in a heading tag will be automatically stylized by a browser according to their default style sheet. Typically, headings are stylized with bigger and thicker font size.

A few of the things you might want to enclosed in heading tags are your website's name, article's title, or article's sub headings. By the way, the <h1> tag is the most important and the <h6> tag is the least important. Usually, a website's name is enclosed in <h1>, the article's title on the page is enclosed in <h2>, and the article's sub headings are enclosed in <h3>. For example:

```
<h1>My Website</h1>

<h2>About the Site</h2>

<p>Place your introductory paragraph here.</p>

<h3>History</h3>

<p>Next paragraph about your website's
history</p>
```

It will appear like this on your browser:

My Website

About the Site

Place your introductory paragraph here.

History

Next paragraph about your website's history

Note that you should not use the heading tags as a mean to bold or enlarge some parts of your text in your document. The reason? The usage of headings is important in web page development, especially if you aim to garner more visitors on your page. Technically, search engines use crawlers (or small programs that read web pages) to index or categorize web pages. Those small applications check and try to understand your page's contents in order to present it to searchers in case your page's content is relevant to what they are searching.

Search engines put more weigh, in terms of relevance, on your page's headings' content more than the paragraphs embedded on the page (that is not how crawlers exactly works, but that is just a basic idea on how they operate). On the other hand, headings raise the readability of your page and define clearly your page's structure.

Keep in mind that the <head> tag is different from headings. Remember that the head tag is used to contain meta data for your web page while the heading tags are used to create emphasis on important texts (or elements) in your document.

Paragraphs

The <p> tag has been mentioned a few times in the previous chapters. And as you have read, the <p> tag is generally used when inserting paragraphs in your web page. When using the <p> tag, you are not restricted on placing text alone in it. You can also insert images and links, or any element that you might want to be included on your paragraph.

By the way, The browser will display the content of your <p> tag from left to right, and will only place the next parts of the content if the text has filled the line. If you want to break your paragraph in the end or start of a specific position, it is recommended that you insert the <br> tag. For example:

```
<p>This is an example paragraph. If you want
to place the last part of this sentence on the
next line, place a <br> tag.</p>
```

This is how it will be displayed on your browser.

This is an example paragraph. If you want to place the last part of this sentence on the next line, place a tag.

The <br> tag does not need to have a closing tag. Browsers automatically place any element after the <p> tag on the next line since it is a block level element (it will be discussed later). If you place a picture after the </p> closing tag, the picture will be placed on the next line.

Also, take note that not only browsers trim trailing spaces, but they also trim consecutive line breaks. If ever you want to add two extra lines within your paragraph, it is best to use two consecutive <br> tags (

).

Another thing that you must be aware of is that the <p> tag will work without a closing tag. For example:

```
<p>Test paragraph. </p>
```

```
<p>Test paragraph 2. </p>
```

The previous lines will produce the same result as:

Test paragraph.

Test paragraph 2.

However, inserting paragraphs in your page like this is not recommendable. You can expect that errors or incorrect display of your page will happen if you use the <p> tag like that.

Basic Formatting

There will be times that you would want to make solid statements in your paragraphs by bolding, italicizing, or highlighting some lines. Alternatively, you might want to place a text as a subscript or a superscript or imply that you updated your article by adding or deleting some lines. Those things are achievable by using the text formatting tags such as <b>, <i>, <strong>, <em>, <mark>, <sub>, <sup>, <ins>, and <del>. You can just nest those tags inside your <p> tag or just enclosed the text you want to format on them.

Bolding and Italicization

In case you want to bold your text, you can use either <b> or <strong>. It is advisable that you use <strong> instead of <b> if you are emphasizing a line. Even though browsers on computers render text enclosed on those two in bold, both have different uses. The <b> tag only makes a text look thicker while the <strong> tag implies that the line is important.

In mobile browsers, it is typical that most text is rendered as bold due to the smallness of the screens of mobile phones. So, if you bold a line in your article and a mobile phone browser displays it, it will not stand out since all the text around it will be bold. In case you use <strong>, the mobile browser may display it differently. Some may thicken the text inside the <strong> tag more; some may enlarge it, while some may display it in all capitals.

On the other hand, the usage of <strong> for emphasized text is also essential for those people who use text-to-speech programs to browse the web. They are commonly those people who are visually impaired and rely on audio to 'read' the contents of your web page. In case their text-to-speech program recognized a line of text that was placed inside the <strong> tag, the program will read it with a different inflection, tone, or volume. On the other hand, if it sees a bold text, it will just read it like any other lines of the text in the article.

The same goes with the usage of <i> and <em>. The two tags make browsers render text as italicized, but only <em> indicates that the text must be emphasized. Bottom line, if you only aim to bold or italicize for the sake of making your lines a bit fancy, use <b> or <i>. If you want to put stress or emphasis on a line, use <strong> or <em> tags instead.

Mark, Sub, Sup, and Small

If you want to mark or highlight text, use <mark>. If you want to subscript or superscript a word or line, use <sub> or <sup>. If you want a line to appear smaller than the others, use <small>. The <small> tag is useful for adding side comments in your article.

Ins and Del

In case you will update your article, it is advisable to take advantage of <ins> and <del> tags. It does not do much to your favor or your website's; however, it will make it easier for your visitors to keep track of the changes you make. By the way, browsers put an underline on those text inside the <ins> tag, and they out a strikethrough on those text inside the <del> tag.

Attributes

HTML is not all about tags and content. To bring a much colorful and more functional web page, you will need to insert attributes on your HTML tags. Attributes are the properties of your tags. Attributes describe how your tag will behave. They can also add more information on the element that you want to insert. By the way, void elements have attributes, too.

For example, you can add the title attribute to a p tag.

```
<p title='About Dogs'>Dogs are man's best
friend. They are lovable. They mostly aim to
please. And if you love them, they will return
your love tenfold. </p>
```

If you place your mouse pointer over that paragraph in your web page, a tooltip will pop-up and it will have the text 'About Dogs'. Some attributes are optional while some must be placed in order for a tag to function the way they need to.

For example, you cannot create a working hyperlink without placing the href attribute in your a HTML tag.

```
<a href='http://www.google.com'>Link to
Google.com</a>
```

In case you forget to indicate the target page in the href attribute of your <a> tag, the content of the tag will not be underlined or clickable – technically, it will not redirect the user since there is no target mentioned.

And the same rule applies to <img> tag. If you do not indicate a src attribute in it, it will not display a picture. It is still possible to create a hyperlink or display a picture without using attributes in your <a> or <img> tags, but it will not be discussed in this book.

As you can see on the examples, it is not that hard to add attributes. All you need to do is include it inside the starting tag's Chevrons. Do not forget to make sure that the tag must be written first and the tag and the attribute must be separated by a space. The value of the attribute that you will assign must be placed after an equals sign and must be enclosed inside single quotes (') or double quotes ("). Even if you are going to assign a number, make sure that you place it inside them.

When writing HTML, make sure that you stick on using either single quotes or double quotes when assigning values to your attributes. Sticking to one allows you to debug or find typographical errors in your document easier. Most HTML developers and HTML development applications stick to using double quotes when assigning values to attributes and using single quotes when placing another value inside the value placed inside the double quotes.

For example:

```
<p title="About Marshall Bruce 'Eminem'
Mathers III" ></p>
```

If the double quote is important, you can interchange the double quotes and single quotes.

```
<p title='About Marshall Bruce "Eminem"
Mathers III' ></p>
```

In case you want to adhere strictly on using double quotes only, but you still want to use double quotes in the attributes value, you can use the ASCII decimal equivalent of the double quote.

```
<p title="About Marshall Bruce
&#34;Eminem&#34; Mathers III" ></p>
```

Never forget to place the ampersand and pound sign before the number and the semicolon at the end when inserting ASCII decimals on your document. Since the ASCII decimal of the double quote is 34, " was used in the previous example.

More on ASCII Characters

Some ASCII characters can be inserted by using the set HTML name for them instead of using the decimal number. Instead of using " to print a double quote, you can use ". The browser will still recognize it. However, not all characters in ASCII have an HTML name.

Some of the HTML names that you will find convenient are:

- " for (")
- & for (&)
- < for (<)
- > for (>)
-   for non breaking spaces

Since the less than and greater than signs are used for tags, problems may occur if you use them in your document. For example, if you accidentally place any text between the less than and the greater than sign, that text will not appear since the browser will consider it as an HTML tag. To prevent that, it is best that you use ASCII when you need to insert any of those two in your page's content.

By the way, browsers automatically truncate any trailing spaces on your document. In case that you have written two consecutive spaces, the browser will only print one. In case that it is important for you to show two, you can take advantage of non breaking spaces. Instead of placing two spaces you can write   instead.

On the other hand, you can get away with not placing quotes around the values you assign. However, this practice will only make your document prone to errors.

By the way, you can assign values to multiple values in one go. Just make sure that you separate them with spaces properly. Also, take note that the attributes that you change will only affect the tag where you specified those attributes.

Links

Links are vital parts of a web page. It allows your user to move around your website and access external web pages without the need of going to the address bar and typing out the address of the page they need to access.

To place a link in your document, you will need to use the <a> tag. There are two things you need to place in the <a> tag for it to be a functional link. First, you will need to indicate the target address where the link will redirect the user who will click it. Second, you will need to indicate the text, image, or element that will serve as the hyperlink.

To indicate the target address, you will need to assign the target address as a value of the <a> tag's href attribute. On the other hand, just type the text between the starting and closing <a> tag. For example:

```
<a href="http://www.google.com" >Google</a>
```

By the way, text hyperlinks are automatically styled by browsers. By default, hyperlinks are underlined and will be colored blue. In case that the user has already clicked that link before, its font will be colored purple. If the user hovers his mouse over the link, it will colored red and his mouse icon will be changed into the little hand icon.

Anyway, never forget to place http:// (https:// if the target page is a secure website or ftp:// if the target page is an FTP directory) on the target address. If you do not, the address will be considered located at the HTML file's local directory (in your computer if the file is in your computer or in the hosting server if the file is uploaded to your website's server).

Target Attribute

You have the option to determine where the target page will be displayed on the user's browser. You can set it to be opened on a new window, a new tab, or the same tab where your user is. You can do that by using the target attribute. There are five values you can place on the target attribute. And they are: _blank, _self, _parent, _top, and "framename".

If you assign _blank, the target page will open in a new window or tab. If you assign _self, the target page will open in the same page where the user clicked the link. By default, the target attribute is set to _self.

On the other hand, if you are working with frames, which will be discussed later, you can use the _parent, _top, and "framename" values. They will be discussed in the frames chapter.

Images

Inserting pictures or images in your web page is as simple as placing a link. To insert one, you will need to use the <img> tag. By the way, the <img> tag is a void element – meaning, you will not need to place a closing tag for it. To indicate which picture you want to insert, you will need to place the src attribute and indicate the location of the image as its value inside the <img> tag. Below is an example:

```
<img
src="http://www.yourwebsite.com/pictures/pictu
re.jpg" >
```

Take note, never forget to indicate the file extension of the picture in the src attribute. The <img> tag can let you display JPEG, GIF, and PNG image files.

If your GIF file has an animation, you do not need to do anything special to make it work in your web page. The browser will automatically play GIF animations that you include in your page. The same goes for PNG or GIF files with alpha masks or transparency.

Image File Locations

You might commonly get your pictures from three locations. The first location is the folder where your picture is located together with your HTML file. The second location is a folder inside a subfolder in the folder where your HTML file is located. And the third location is a parent folder of your HTML file's folder or webpage on another website.

In case the picture file you want to insert is together with the HTML file in the same folder, you do not need to indicate the full address of the picture. Its filename will suffice. For example:

```
<img src="picture.jpg" >
```

If the picture is within a subfolder inside the folder where your HTML is located, you can just indicate the folder name and then the filename. For example, if the subfolder's name is picturesfolder, the src attribute's value will look like this:

```
<img src="picturesfolder/picture.jpg" >
```

In the event that the picture is on another website, it will be best to place the full address of the picture in the src attribute.

```
<img
src="http://www.yourwebsite.com/pictures/pictu
re.jpg" >
```

If the picture is on the parent folder of the folder where your HTML file resides, you can do this instead:

```
<img src="../picture.jpg" >
```

The "../" means that the file parser must check the previous folder for the file. You can stack two of them if your HTML file's folder is two levels or folders deep away from the parent folder that holds the picture file. You can also do that practice with links or anything with the href attribute.

Alt Attribute

There will be times that the image you want to insert might go offline or might not load. When any of those happens, you can let the browser replace the image with a text as a placeholder by using the alt tag. For example:

```
<img src="http://www.yourwebsite.com/pictures/picture.jpg" alt="This is a picture." >
```

Placing alt text on images has numerous advantages. One of them is to let search engines index the image on their database. Second, visually impaired users will be able to have an idea of the picture you inserted. Remember that they use text-to-speech programs to browse. And those programs are not capable of reading or describing pictures to their users without checking the values of the images' alt attribute.

Another reminder, alt text must be always placed on your <img> tags in order for your file to be validated without any problems.

Basic Image Resizing

When you insert a picture in your HTML file, whatever its size will be displayed on the page. Of course, there will be times that you would want to resize big pictures to become smaller and vice versa. You can do that by using the width and height attribute. Below is an example:

```
<img
src="http://www.yourwebsite.com/pictures/pictu
re.jpg" alt="This is a picture." width="100px"
height="100px" >
```

The attributes will force your picture to be displayed with a dimension of 100px by 100px. If the picture is bigger than the dimension you set, the browser will shrink it. Alternatively, if the picture is smaller, it will be stretched. By the way, px means pixels. It is one of the standard measurements that you will be using a lot in HTML development.

Style Attribute

On the other hand, there is another method you can use to resize or scale the size of the picture you will insert. And that is the style attribute. However, unlike the width and height attributes, the style attribute can be used to modify the overall appearance of an element, which will be discussed later. Anyway, below is an example on how to use the style attribute in resizing an image.

```
<img
src="http://www.yourwebsite.com/pictures/pictu
re.jpg" alt="This is a picture."
style="width:100px;height:100px;" >
```

You might have already have an idea on how to use it by seeing an example. But it will be discussed fully later.

In case that you have placed a broken URL or you made a mistake in typing the source image that you want to display, the browser will render a small icon (usually, it is a broken picture icon) and the alt text you placed.

Tables

Tables make it easier for HTML developers to display lists on their websites. Other than that, tables have been used adamantly back then as a styling container. However, with the development of container elements and CSS, tables have been rarely used for any other purpose except to display lists.

The <table> element contains three more elements. And they are <th>, <tr>, and <td>. The <th> tag defines the table's headers. The <tr> tag defines the table's row/s. The <td> tag defines the table's data cell/s.

When making a table, do not forget that the three elements must be nested on the right places for the browser to display a proper table. For you to have an idea, below is an example:

```
<table border="1" >

    <tr>
```

```
    <td>Cell 1</td>

    <td>Cell 2</td>

  </tr>

</table>
```

The example will produce a 2 x 1 table like this:

Cell 1	Cell 2

By the way, notice that a border attribute was placed on the <table> tag. In case you do not place a value for that attribute or not include it, the browsers will not display any borders, which might confuse you. Also, the appearance of the table may vary from browser to browser.

The number of <td> tags you place inside the <tr> tags determine the number of columns that your table will have. Also, by the default, the table will automatically adjust its size to fit in all the contents that you have placed in the <td> and <th> tags.

If you want to add more rows, just add more <tr> tags and fill them with <td> tags. On the other hand, if you want to add table headers, create a row filled with <th> tags. Below is an example.

```
<table border="1" >

    <tr>

        <th>Column 1 Header</td>

        <th>Column 2 Header</td>

    </tr>

    <tr>

        <td>Cell 1</td>

        <td>Cell 2</td>

    </tr>

    <tr>

        <td>Cell 3</td>

        <td>Cell 4</td>

    </tr>

</table>
```

Column 1 Header	Column 2 Header
Cell 1	Cell 2
Cell 3	Cell 4

In case you do not prefer to place your headers on top of columns and want them to be located in the first column instead, you can just place the <th> tags as the first element inside the <tr> tag.

The <td> and <th> do not differ that much. The only difference between them is that the content inside the <th> tags are styled. Nevertheless, it will be always a good practice to use the right tag for the right content.

By the way, you can insert paragraph, links, images, and almost any other elements aside from meta elements inside the <td> tags.

Lists

Of course, you would not want to use tables for small lists. The <ul> and/or <ol> tags are the better choice. The <ul> tag stands for unordered list, and the <ol> tag stands for ordered list. They function the same, but have one difference. The <ul> list your items with bullets while the <ol> tag list your items with numbers, letters, or roman letters.

To add an item to your list, you will need to use the <li> or list item tag. It should be nested inside <ul> or <ol>. Below are examples:

```
<ul>
```

```
    <li>Dog</li>

    <li>Cat</li>

    <li>Mouse</li>

</ul>
```

That unordered list will appear like this:

- Dog
- Cat
- Mouse

```
<ol>

    <li>Denial</li>

    <li>Anger</li>

    <li>Bargaining</li>

    <li>Depression</li>

    <li>Acceptance</li>

</ol>
```

That ordered list will appear like this:

1. Denial

2. Anger

3. Bargaining

4. Depression

5. Acceptance

List Style Type

With the <ol> tag, you can change the numbers with letters and roman numerals. You can do that by placing the type attribute inside the tag. The values you can input in the type attribute are:

1 – this is set by default and will place numbers on your ordered list.

A – using this will change the numbers into capital letters.

a – on the other hand, this will let the ordered list use small letters instead.

I – placing this value will set the ordered list to using capital roman numerals.

i – and just like with the small a this will display small roman numerals.

Below is an example:

```
<ol type="I">

    <li>Denial</li>

    <li>Anger</li>

    <li>Bargaining</li>

    <li>Depression</li>

    <li>Acceptance</li>
</ol>
```

I.   Denial

II.   Anger

III.   Bargaining

IV.   Depression

V.   Acceptance

The same can be applied to the unordered list. However, instead of numbers and letters, you can change the shape or symbol that will appear beside your list items. Some of the values you can place on the type attribute of the <ul> tag are:

- disc (this is the default value and will place bullets in your list)

- o circle

- ▪ square

none – this will remove the symbol that comes with the <ul> tag.

List Child

You can also place child lists inside your list. All you need to do is to nest another <ol> or <ul> after the <li> tag where you want to place the child list. Below is an example:

```
<ul>
    <li>Dog</li>
    <ul>
        <li>Bulldog</li>
        <li>Siberian Husky</li>
        <li>Bichon Frise</li>
    </ul>
    <li>Cat</li>
    <li>Mouse</li>
</ul>
```

This will be the result.

- Dog
    - Bulldog
    - Siberian Husky
    - Bichon Frise
- Cat
- Mouse

Aside from using the <ul> and <ol> tags for lists, they are also used in creating menus and navigation bars. When you learn CSS, you will know how to change the usual vertical listings into horizontal listings (this is what web developers usually do to create a navigation bar).

Description List

Aside from the <ul> and <ol> tags, you can use the <dl> or description list tag to create a list with heavy emphasis on definitions. This type of list is usually used in dictionary and thesaurus sites. Below is an example:

```
<dl>
    <dt>Dog</dt>
```

```
    <dd>- man's best friend</dd>

    <dt>Cat</dt>

    <dd>- man's best friend's mortal
enemy</dd>

    <dt>Mouse</dt>

    <dd>- mortal enemy of the cat </dd>
</dl>
```

Dog

   - man's best friend

Cat

   - man's best friend's mortal enemy

Mouse

   - mortal enemy of the cat

Instead of using the <li> tag to include a list item, you will need to use <dt> or the description term. To place the description of the term you placed, you will need to use <dd> or data description (not really the meaning of the tag, but it can help you remember it).

Adding Comments

If you are going to write hundreds of lines in your web page document, you might easily get lost in doing it, especially if you will need a few days before you finish it.

Even though basic text editors have search function, you might get stumped if you cannot recall the term you wanted to search. Because of that, it is advantageous to sprinkle some comments in your document.

Adding comments in a large web page, is good practice that can allow you see visual reminders of what you need to do, what you have done, and why you have done or added some stuff in your document.

To add a comment, you can just place it between the start comment tag, which is <!—and the end tag -->. For example:

```
<!-- This is an example comment. -->
```

By the way, you can place comments almost everywhere in your web document. But of course, you would not want to place them together with attributes. Also, comments will not appear on the page when you load your document on a browser. In addition, you can create multiple lines of comments.

On the other hand, comments are not only good as visual markers, but they can also function as a method to disable any content or element to appear in your document temporarily.

By the way, do not place a comment inside a comment. The first instance of a closing comment tag will terminate the comment. For example:

```
<!-- This is a comment <!-- This is a comment
inside a comment --> -->
```

The first --> closing tag will terminate the comment. And due to that, the last --> will be recognize as content, and will be printed on the web page.

On HTML editors, comments are usually highlighted with green font.

Chapter 3: A Quick and Condense Discussion about CSS

Technically, this part of the book will cover CSS (Cascading Style Sheets). CSS is primarily used to change the appearance of your web page and each element in it. And there are three ways to do that:

1. Using the style attribute inside an element tag.

2. Declaring CSS values in the <style> tag.

3. And creating a separate CSS file and linking it in the web page.

The Style Attribute or Inline Styles

Below is an example of the first method:

```
<p style="color:blue;" >The color of the text
in this paragraph will become blue.</p>
```

The color of the text in this paragraph will become blue.

You can think of the style attribute as an attribute holder. Technically, color is an attribute or CSS property of the <p>

tag. To assign a value to that property, you will need to place a colon after it, and then place the value that you want to assign. Since the property color determines the font color of the paragraph, you would want to place a color value, which on that example was blue.

There are multiple CSS properties that you can use in order to customize your elements. Also, you can place multiple CSS property assignments in the style attribute. Just make sure that you separate them with a semicolon. By the way, the semicolon on the end is not necessary. Below is an example:

```
<p style="color:blue;font-size:20px;" >The
color of the text in this paragraph will
become blue and will become bigger.</p>
```

The color of the text in this paragraph will become blue and will become bigger.

The Style Tag or Internal Stylesheet

In case that you will need to change the style of multiple elements, using the <style> tag will be a much better choice. After all, if you are going to place a style attribute in every element in your web page, your code will become messy and you will be wasting a lot of time, especially if you are going to change the same attribute with the same value in the same elements.

The style tag is considered a meta element. And that means that you must place it in the head tag. When it comes to using the style tag, there are five ways to change the value of an element or elements' CSS properties.

Styling Using the Element's Name as a Selector

Below is an example of how to do CSS in the style tag by using this first method:

```
<head>

<style>

p {

color:blue;

font-size:20px;

}

</style>

</head>
```

In this example, all the contents in all the <p> tags in your web page will be colored blue and will have a font size of 20px. This is a broad way of using CSS. And it is advantageous if you are planning to style all elements with one unified style.

By the way, the CSS syntax is much different from HTML and it might confuse you at first. But it is rather simple to be honest. There are two parts in a CSS line. The first part is the selector. On the example, the selector used was p, which means that the browser will target all the <p> elements.

The second part is the declaration, which should be enclosed with curly brackets. The declaration is separated into four parts. The first part is the CSS property, which on the example is blue. The second part is the colon, which indicates that the value of the property will come next. The third part is the value itself, which on the example is blue. And the fourth part is the declaration separator, which is the semi comma.

By the way, you do not need to create a new line for every declaration. You can declare and assign values to those CSS properties in succession – just like assigning CSS values in the style attribute.

Styling Using the Element's ID as a Selector

Using the element tag's name could be too broad for you. And there will be times that you just want to style one element in your document. In this case, you will need to select the element to style by using its ID.

By the way, the element ID can be assigned by declaring the id attribute. Below is an example:

```
<p id="firstparagraph" >This is the first
paragraph</p>
```

Take note that to assign a valid id to an element, the id must not start with a number. Anyway, to style that paragraph, you will need to use its ID as the selector in your CSS declaration.

```
<head>

<style>

#firstparagraph {

color:blue;

font-size:20px;

}

</style>

</head>
```

Notice that there is a pound sign included in the selector. The pound sign denotes that you are going to use an id selector. If you do not put it, it will not work since the browser will think that you are trying to select all instances of an element named firstparagraph.

Styling Using Class as a Selector

But what if you want to style two or more specific elements, but want to leave the others intact? In that case, you will need to use classes as selectors. Just like the id attribute, you can include an element into one class by declaring it inside the starting tag of an element. Below is an example:

```
<p class="blueparagraphs" >This will be one of
the few blue colored paragraphs.</p>
```

By the way, the class attribute is a bit flexible. You can include an element in one or more classes by separating each class names inside the class attribute. Also, you can include different elements in one class. Below is an example:

```
<p class="blueparagraphs bigfont" >This will
be one of the few blue colored paragraphs. And
will be included in the textelements
class.</p>
```

```
<h1 class=" bigfont" >This header is also
included in the bigfont class.</h1>
```

To use class as the selector, you will need to place a dot before the name of the class on your CSS declaration. Take note of the example below:

```
<head>

<style>

.bigfont {

font-size:40px;

}


.blueparagraphs {
```

```
color:blue;

}

</style>

</head>
```

Take note that this CSS declaration will affect all elements included in the bigfont class, which means that the p and h1 included on it will have a font size of 40px. By the way, as you can see in the previous example, you can place multiple CSS declaration in the <style> tag – just make sure that you follow the proper syntax.

Styling Using the Element Tag and Class as a Selector

However, in case that you just want to target all the <p> tags in the bigfont class and avoid changing the style of the <h1> tag in the bigfont class, you can narrow your selector down by using an element tag together with the class. All you need to do is indicate the tag's name as the selector and follow it up with a dot and the name of the class. An example is below:

```
<head>

<style>

p.bigfont {
```

```
font-size:40px;

}

</style>

</head>
```

Styling Using the Group Selectors

In case you want to style multiple elements or just want certain type of elements to have the same CSS properties or property, you can use group selectors. Not only it will save your time, but it will make your CSS lines cleaner. For example:

```
<head>

<style>

p, h1 {

color:red;

}

</style>

</head>
```

In that example, all contents inside the <p> and <h1> tags will have a red font. To make sure that your CSS declaration using group selectors to work, never forget to separate each element name with a comma. You can also do group selection with ids and classes – just make sure that you do not forget the pound and dot symbols respectively.

In case you did not do a CSS group selection, the previous example might have looked like this:

```
<head>

<style>

p {

color:red;

}


h1 {

color:red;

}

</style>

</head>
```

As you can see, not using group selectors is a wee bit uneconomical.

Using a Separate File for CSS or External Style Sheet

There are three reasons you should place your CSS declarations on a separate file. First, putting it on a separate file makes your web page's code clean and less cluttered. Second, you can use the CSS files on multiple pages. In case you will have pages that will have a uniformed design, a CSS file is a must. Third, coding is much less confusing since HTML and CSS have different syntaxes and setting them apart makes coding a bit easier.

To create a separate CSS file, just create a new file with a .css extension. Any file name will do as long as you do not forget to indicate the right file extension. You can use notepad for that. After that, type all the CSS declarations you want to implement on your web page. By the way, you do not need to enclose the declaration with the <style> tag anymore. Just place or type the declarations and save the file.

Of course, the browser will not know if your web page will need the CSS file that you just created. Because of that, you will need to declare it in your code. To do that, you will need to use the <link> tag. Below is an example on how you will link the CSS file you created into your web page:

```
<head>
```

```
<link rel="stylesheet" type="text/css"
href="MyCSSFile.css">

</head>
```

By the way, just like the <style> tag, the <link> tag is another meta element, which means it should be placed on the <head> tag. The <link> tag is also a void element that does not need a closing tag. Also, do not confuse the <link> tag with the <a> anchor tag.

In the example above, you can see three attributes: rel, type, and href. You might already have an idea on the href's role, which is to indicate the location of your CSS file. The rel attribute is there for you to state the relationship between your webpage and the CSS file. In this case, stylesheet should be assigned to it. And the type attribute will contain the information about what kind of document you are linking to your page.

Multiple CSS Links and Declarations

It is possible to link multiple CSS files in one web page. Also, using all the CSS declaration methods will work in one web page. However, take note that there is a priority hierarchy that a browser would follow when it comes to CSS. If there are multiple instances of CSS property value changes for one or more elements in the document and CSS files, the browser will follow the last declaration or changes.

For you to get the idea, below is the priority hierarchy with one being the highest and four being the lowest:

1. Inline Style

2. Internal Style

3. External Style

4. Browser Style

And yes; browsers have their own default style sheets. Whenever you do not change a CSS property value, the browser will follow its own style sheet.

In case you have placed this:

```
#paragraph1 {

color:red;

}
```

on your external style sheet but placed this in your page's body:

```
<p id="paragraph1" style="color:blue;" >Test
Paragraph</p>
```

The browser will display that paragraph in blue font.

But just to be clear, if you placed this:

```
#paragraph1 {

color:red;

font-size:20px;

}
```

and then placed this on your document's body:

```
<p id="paragraph1" style="color:blue;" >Test
Paragraph</p>
```

The paragraph will still have the blue font, but it will still get the 20px font size since nothing else overridden the font-size value after it was declared.

CSS Properties and Compatibility

It would be fun and more educating if every CSS properties will be discussed here. However, there are tons of them! And it can even be safely said that CSS properties outnumber HTML tags – not to mention that some properties differ for each browser. Also, some properties do not work on other browsers or their previous versions.

Due to that, when learning CSS, always keep a reference list ready. Also, put in mind browser and device compatibility when starting to do advanced CSS stuff. The design that you might create and view on your computer screen might not appear the same on other computers, browsers, or devices.

Chapter 4: Last Things You Need to Know

Block and Inline Level Elements

Element tags can be again categorized into two. The first one is block level elements. And the second one is inline level elements.

Block level elements, when displayed on a browser, are always sandwiched between two new lines. One perfect example of a block level element is <p>, <table>, and heading tags. Below is an example:

```
<p>This is one paragraph.</p><p>And this is
another.</p>
```

This is one paragraph.

And this is another.

As you can see, a new line was automatically produced after the first <p> tag.

On the other hand, inline level elements do not have that same treatment from browsers. The browser will just display them without any line breaks or spaces after them. Good examples are <img> and <a> tags. Below is an example:

```
<a href="none.htm" >Broken link.</a><a
href="none.htm" >Broken link 2.</a>
```

Broken link.Broken link 2.

Changing from Block to Inline and Vice Versa

There will be times that you will want a block element to become an inline because you want to get rid of the extra new lines. One good reason to change a block to an inline level element is when changing the direction of a <list> tag to horizontal, which is useful when creating a navigation bar.

Grouping Tags and HTML5 Semantic Tags

There will be times that your web page will contain a lot of content, and it will become too messy to handle or to display the way you want in a browser. Due to that, you should take advantage of grouping tags such as <div> and <span>. These two tags' primary purpose is to contain other elements or tags. By the way, the <div> tag is a block element while the <span> tag is inline.

When the two were not yet were popular, the <table> tag was used instead to contain other elements. And a while back, when the HTML5 standards were not yet widespread, most web developers rely on the <div> and <span> tags to build the structure of their pages – to the point that the presence of <div> tags have outnumbered the number of other elements in their pages. Some web developers even called it a worse case of "divititis".

Nowadays, web page makers are advocated to take advantage of the new semantic tags introduced in HTML5. Some of those semantic tags are:

- <header>

- <section>

- <nav>

- <article>

- <figure>

- <aside>

- <footer>

- <figcaption>

- <summary>

- <details>

- <time>

- <mark>

Instead of using <div> to contain all the elements in your navigation bar, you can use the <nav> tag instead.

Benefits of Semantic Tags versus Grouping Tags

First of all, the code of your page will be much readable. You will not need to add comments just to remind you where your headings or navigation links are.

Second, styling semantic tags are much easier than styling multiple <div> and <span> tags by using their element IDs or classes. Even though this might be a small issue for veterans, it could greatly help new web publishers who are not yet masters of CSS.

SEO and Semantic Tags

There have been a lot of rumors that the semantic tags introduced in HTML5 can help websites gain more SEO ranking. Truth be told, this is unproven. First of all, even a website that uses <table> tags to structure its pages can rank higher than those who are using semantic tags to arrange and structure their elements.

However, even if that is the case, it will be much better to take advantage of semantic tags since you will never know when search engines will consider those elements in their future algorithms.

Basic Web Page Structure

You might have already visited hundreds of websites before you read this. And you must already have an idea on how websites are structured.

On the top of the page, you will see the header bar. It contains the website's title and logo usually. Sometimes you will see the page's own title or header inside it.

After the header bar is the navigation bar. The navigation bar contains links to other important pages on a website. In the middle of the page, you will find the main content area. It contains the article, blog posts, and image galleries.

And at the bottom, you will find the footer. Links to copyright notices, website policies, etc. are usually placed there.

Below is a short example of code. It will produce a page with the simplest structure. And in the future, it is possible that you will use it as your main template.

```
<!DOCTYPE html>

<html>

<head>

<title>My First Web Page</title>

<style>
```

```
li {

display:inline;

}


footer {

text-align:center;

}

</style>

</head>


<body>


<header>

<h1>This is my site!</h1>

</header>


<nav>

    <ul>

        <li><a href="index.htm" >Home</a>

        <li><a href="about.htm" >About</a>
```

```html
        <li><a href="contact.htm" >Contact Us</a>

    </ul>

</nav>


<main>

    <article>

        <h1>Welcome to My Website!</h1>

        <p>Hello. Insert tons of paragraphs here.</p>

    </article>

</main>


<footer>

    <ul>

        <li><a href="terms.htm" >Terms of Service</a>

        <li><a href="privacy.htm" >Privacy Policies</a>

        <li><a href="help.htm" >Help</a>

    </ul>
```

```
</footer>

</body>

</html>
```

It is not that hard, right? All you need now is to fill up all the necessary elements and contents inside that template, and you will have a decent web page.

If you want to make it appear cooler, just learn more CSS properties and apply it to your page. On the other hand, you should also get an HTML tag list ready. There are a lot of elements that were not covered here. Some are essential some are not. Nevertheless, congratulations on covering all the basics. Good luck.

Conclusion and for Further Learning

Woah! You have reached the last part of this book. By this time, you already have an idea on how to create a decent web page. Most probably, you are a bit disappointed. Your website does not look like what you always see on the web. You might think that your site looks so retro and boring.

However, remember that you are only in the starting point of web development. You only have the basic idea on the fundamentals of creating websites. You will use the knowledge you gained here all the time when you advance to the next level of web publishing. After all, HTML is a prerequisite to almost anything web development related.

A Quick Discussion on Static Pages

The pages you will create from this point forward are considered static HTML or web page. Just as its name implies, a static page's content do not change. Even if you input anything on it, any element on it will be left unchanged. Alternatively, a page that has content that changes is called a dynamic page. For example, the front page of a news website like CNN or New York Times changes every day.

A Quick Discussion on Responsive Pages and Client Side Scripting

The next type of web pages you would want to develop or create are responsive web pages. They are web pages that do something when you interact with it. For example, clicking on a button will make a popup box appear. Or clicking on a box will make it disappear, change it size, or make a text appear inside it.

And for you to create that kind of web pages, you will need to learn client side scripting. You will need to study JavaScript. After that, advance your client side scripting mastery by learning JScript. By the way, learning CSS3 is also a plus when learning client side scripting. Also, be a bit wary; unlike HTML coding, client side scripting will make you use some programming skills. But you will surely get the hang of it fast.

A Quick Discussion on Dynamic Pages and Server Side Scripting

When you viewed some web pages on the internet, you might have asked yourself if it is possible for you to create pages like that by using Notepad? Well, the answer is yes – design wise; however, as of now, it will be impossible for you to create a page that can interact with a user and provide dynamic content (changing content).

In case you have started to check the sources or HTML codes of web pages that you frequently access, you might have noticed that of them appear as a pile of random text and numbers. It might be difficult for you to see or comprehend how it was created by writing HTML. A good example is a page inside your Facebook account. Try opening one right now.

The reason that the source of one of your Facebook's account page is a mess is because its HTML code was generated by the server – mostly by server side scripting. With server side scripting you will handle more advanced things. You will be tackling server side scripting languages like PHP and ASP. And you will be frequently dealing with database management. In case you did not give up web development after learning client side scripting, server side scripting will be your next step to web development.

www.ingramcontent.com/pod-product-compliance
Lightning Source LLC
Chambersburg PA
CBHW061033050326
40689CB00012B/2799